GARDEN SQUAD!

COMPOSTING

DWAYNE HICKS

PowerKiDS press.

New York

Published in 2016 by The Rosen Publishing Group, Inc.
29 East 21st Street, New York, NY 10010

First Edition

Editor: Sarah Machajewski
Book Design: Michael J. Flynn

Photo Credits: Cover Atelier_A/Shutterstock.com; back cover, pp. 3–4, 6–8, 10–20, 23–24 (soil texture) Andrey_Kuzmin/Shutterstock.com; p. 5 (compost pile) © iStockphoto.com/Allkindza; p. 5 (girl) gorillaimages/Shutterstock.com; p. 7 (manure) Tobias Arhelger/Shutterstock.com; p. 7 (food) audaxl/Shutterstock.com; p. 7 (plants) Witkowski Marcin/Shutterstock.com; p. 7 (wood chips) extender_01/Shutterstock.com; p. 7 (straw) 9nong/Shutterstock.com; p. 7 (leaves) ProKasia/Shutterstock.com; p. 8 (worm) kzww/Shutterstock.com; pp. 9 (humus), 19 (worms) macrovarro/Shutterstock.com; p. 9 (bacteria) Sashkin/Shutterstock.com; p. 11 Joan Ramon Mendo Escoda/Shutterstock.com; p. 12 (compost bin) Wichien Tepsuttinun/ Shutterstock.com; p. 13 BMJ/Shutterstock.com; p. 15 © iStockphoto.com/thomasmax; p. 17 © iStockphoto.com/nanoqfu; p. 19 (food scraps) mubus7/Shutterstock.com; p. 19 (shoveling) kryzhov/Shutterstock.com; p. 19 (vegetables growing) udra11/Shutterstock.com; p. 19 (vegetable plate) Yulia Davidovich/Shutterstock.com; p. 21 (carrots and cucumbers) K. Decha/ Shutterstock.com; p. 21 (leachate) PRILL/Shutterstock.com; p. 22 Jupiterimages/Photolibrary/ Getty Images.

Cataloging-in-Publication Data

Hicks, Dwayne.
Composting / by Dwayne Hicks.
p. cm. — (Garden squad!)
Includes index.
ISBN 978-1-4994-0945-1 (pbk.)
ISBN 978-1-4994-0965-9 (6 pack)
ISBN 978-1-4994-1010-5 (library binding)
1. Compost — Juvenile literature. I. Hicks, Dwayne. II. Title.
S661.H53 2016
635.9'1875—d23

Manufactured in the United States of America

CPSIA Compliance Information: Batch #WS15PK: For Further Information contact Rosen Publishing, New York, New York at 1-800-237-9932

CONTENTS

DIG IN!

Gardening is a fun outdoor activity. Whether you grow a big vegetable garden or a tiny patch of flowers, working with plants is a great way to understand the natural world while also having fun.

For thousands of years, new and experienced gardeners have shared tips for growing the best plants. Everyone approaches gardening a bit differently, but there's one thing most gardeners agree on: composting is one of the best things you can do! Composting is a **process** that adds **nutrients** to soil. Let's dig in and get our hands dirty by learning about composting.

Kids can compost! It's an easy activity for any age group.

WHAT IS COMPOST?

Composting starts with one thing: compost! This word may be unfamiliar to you. So, what is it? Compost is a mix of green organic matter and brown organic matter. "Organic" means the matter comes from living things, such as plants and animals.

Green matter and brown matter are different. Green matter includes food, grass clippings, and **manure**. Green matter is moist, or wet, and contains a lot of the element nitrogen. Brown matter includes wood chips, leaves, and straw. Brown matter is dry and high in carbon, which is another element. Over time, greens and browns break down and turn into compost.

GARDEN GUIDE

The big mixture of greens and browns is called a compost pile.

MANURE

WOOD CHIPS

FOOD

STRAW

GRASS CLIPPINGS

LEAVES

Brown matter can also include newspaper, cardboard, and dryer lint.

MUNCHING MICROORGANISMS

The first step in composting is mixing greens and browns. Then, nature takes over. Your pile of matter will turn into compost over time with the help of **microorganisms**, which are also known as decomposers.

Fungi and bacteria are your compost's best friends. These tiny creatures love to feed on dead matter, which is exactly what's in your compost pile. As they eat, they unlock **minerals** and nutrients in the dead matter and leave behind humus. Humus is dark brown or black and smells like soil. This end product is what gardeners set out to make when they start composting.

GARDEN GUIDE

Worms are another garden decomposer. They eat rotting matter and leave behind nutrients, which helps improve soil quality.

HUMUS

BACTERIA

Bacteria are tiny creatures that can only be seen with a microscope.

PLAYING WITH NATURE

Though many gardeners take composting into their own hands, this process has been happening naturally for as long as plants have been on Earth. Dead trees and plants that fall to the ground are broken down by microorganisms. They put nutrients back into the soil, which helps new plants grow. The only difference between natural composting and garden composting is you!

There are some things you can do to help your compost pile along. Smaller pieces of matter give microorganisms more surfaces to feed on. Microorganisms need water and oxygen, a gas in the air, to do their job. You can help by keeping your compost moist and turning it over from time to time.

GARDEN GUIDE

Small pieces of matter, water, and oxygen are important to composting, but you don't want too much of

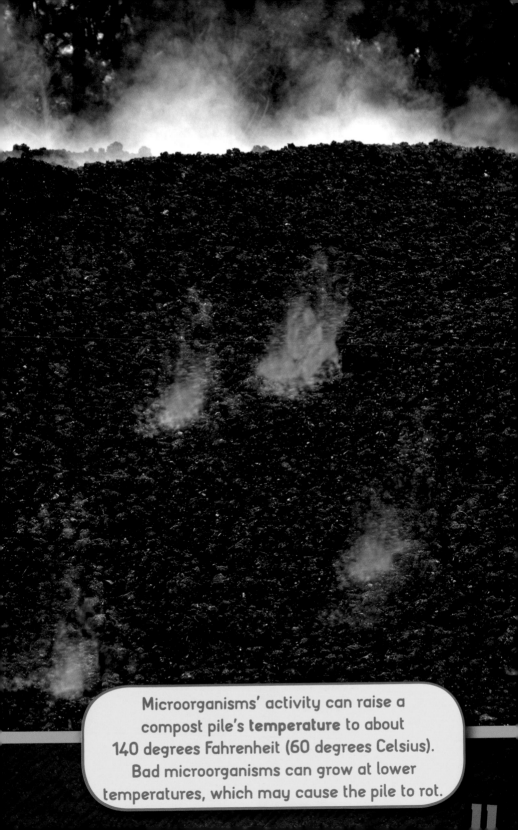

Microorganisms' activity can raise a compost pile's **temperature** to about 140 degrees Fahrenheit (60 degrees Celsius). Bad microorganisms can grow at lower temperatures, which may cause the pile to rot.

GETTING STARTED

Once you're ready to start composting, all it takes is a little bit of effort. Choose a spot in your backyard to begin a compost pile, or use a compost bin. Compost bins are usually covered plastic containers, or objects used to hold something.

Next, start composting! Create equal **layers** of greens and browns. It's important to cover any food scraps with a 10-inch layer of brown matter so animals and bugs don't come by for a meal. Finally, add water and wait! Your compost pile will take a few weeks to change, but you can keep adding matter as you get it.

This is what your compost pile would look like if you cut it down the middle. Notice the equal layers of greens and browns.

GARDEN GUIDE

Backyard compost piles are easy to create, but can be tricky to care for. Make sure they don't get too wet from rain and that animals don't eat your greens. Covering it with plastic can help.

COMPOSTING IN THE KITCHEN

As you make your compost pile, you may wonder if what you have in the kitchen is compostable. Remember this rule: if it's not food, it's not compostable!

Most green matter will come from your kitchen, since food scraps are great for compost piles. This includes apple cores, carrot peelings, orange peels, and lettuce. You can also compost eggs and eggshells, milk, bread, butter, and nuts. Almost anything you can eat can be composted. Plastic, napkins, metal, and glass are not compostable.

Some compostable matter is found outside. Collect grass clippings, leaves, and wood chips when you find them in your yard.

GARDEN GUIDE

Animal manure is a great compost material, but only if it comes from cows or other farm animals. Never use your cat or dog's poop! It contains bacteria that should

IS IT COMPOSTABLE?

NO	YES
PLASTIC	CARROTS
NAPKINS	APPLES
PAPER PLATES	ORANGES
MILK CARTONS	PIZZA
CANS	ICE CREAM
METAL	EGGSHELLS
GLASS	BREAD
JARS	BUTTER
JUICE BOXES	BROCCOLI
	LETTUCE

Some people say not to put meat and bones in your compost pile. Meat can attract lots of pests, including flies, cockroaches, rats, raccoons, and neighborhood pets.

USING "GARDENER'S GOLD"

It can take anywhere from weeks to months to make compost. Once you have this "gardener's gold," how do you use it? Add compost to your garden bed, and watch your plants grow healthy and strong. Mix it into old, dried-out dirt to give your soil a blast of nutrients. Just don't add compost to indoor plants—it may contain weeds and seeds that aren't good to have inside.

Compost helps your garden in many ways. It balances your soil's nutrients, water, and oxygen. It protects plants from common diseases, or sicknesses. It also feeds worms and microorganisms that keep your garden healthy.

GARDEN GUIDE

Every season, plants take nutrients from soil to live and grow. Over time, the soil becomes low in nutrients. Adding compost breathes new life into your soil.

Compost has helped these plants grow.

17

CLOSING THE FOOD CYCLE

Composting isn't just good for your garden. It's also good for the **environment**. Using **fertilizers** puts chemicals on plants and in the ground. People and animals that eat these plants are also eating chemicals. Rainwater may carry chemicals from the soil into our water supply. Composting is a good way to keep our environment and food chemical-free.

Composting also helps the environment because it's a form of recycling. Instead of putting food in the trash, you use it to create healthy soil that will help grow more food. This is called a closed food cycle.

Your garden can be part of a closed food cycle if you use compost.

COLLECT THE FOOD WASTE

FEED TO THE WORMS

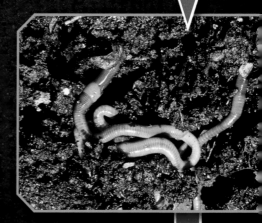

PREPARE AND EAT THE FOOD

ADD COMPOST TO THE SOIL

WHY SHOULD YOU COMPOST?

One of the biggest benefits of composting is that it reduces, or lowers, the amount of waste that goes to **landfills**. Food that goes to landfills can't break down into the ground. Instead, it rots. This puts a gas called methane into the air, which makes Earth warmer than normal. This can have a bad effect on the future of our planet.

Another way landfills harm the planet is by giving off a chemical-filled liquid called leachate. Leachate soaks into the ground and runs off into our streams, lakes, and oceans. This harms animals, plants, and people. Composting means less trash goes to landfills. Smaller landfills mean less methane and leachate and a healthier world.

Composting is one way your tiny garden can help better our world.

LEACHATE

COMPOSTING FOR A BETTER WORLD

There's nothing bad about composting. It's fun, easy, and free. It helps your garden, teaches you about the natural world, and also helps our planet. Now is the time to get started!

Are you ready to compost? Ask an adult to help you choose a place for a compost pile, or buy a compost bin from the store. Separate your food scraps from your garbage, and watch them turn into garden food. At first, you'll see your garden produce healthy, strong plants. In time, our planet will become healthier and stronger, too.

COMPOSTING

GLOSSARY

environment: The natural world in which a plant or animal lives.

fertilizer: A chemical or natural substance added to soil to grow healthier plants.

fungi: Living things that are somewhat like a plant, but don't make their own food, have leaves, or have a green color. Fungi include molds and mushrooms. The singular form is "fungus."

landfill: A place where trash is taken, then crushed down and covered with dirt.

layer: One thickness laying over or under another.

manure: Animal waste used to fertilize crops and gardens.

microorganism: A tiny creature that can only be seen with a microscope.

mineral: Nonliving matter found in nature that's important for animals and plants in small quantities.

nutrient: Something a living thing needs to grow and stay alive.

process: A series of actions or changes.

quality: How good something is.

temperature: How hot or cold something is.

INDEX

WEBSITES

Due to the changing nature of Internet links, PowerKids Press has developed an online list of websites related to the subject of this book. This site is updated regularly. Please use this link to access the list: www.powerkidslinks.com/grdn/comp

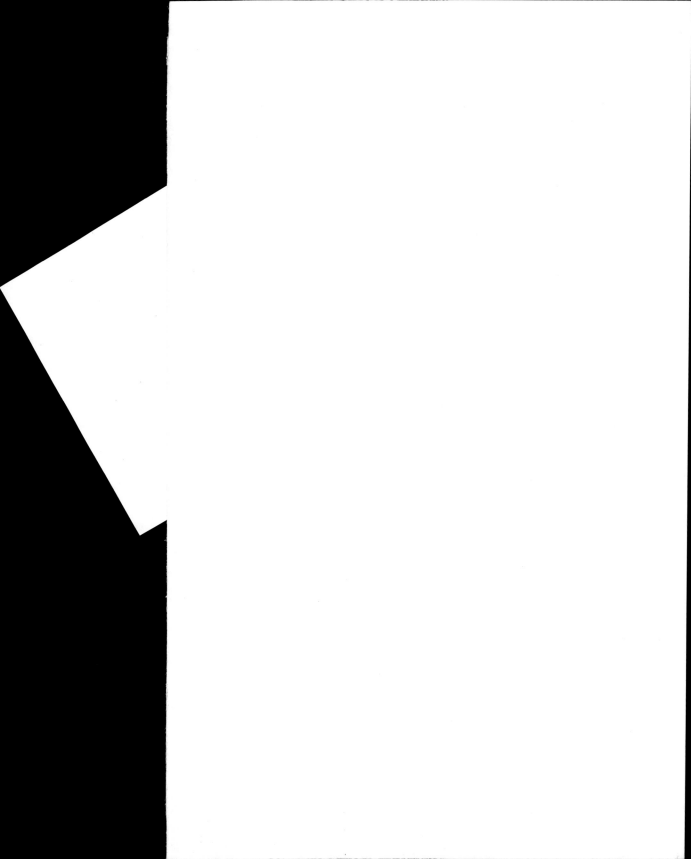

DATE DUE